The Parting of the Red Sea

and other Bible Stories

Retold by Vic Parker

Miles Kelly

First published in 2011 by Miles Kelly Publishing Ltd
Harding's Barn, Bardfield End Green, Thaxted, Essex, CM6 3PX, UK

Copyright © Miles Kelly Publishing Ltd 2011

2 4 6 8 10 9 7 5 3 1

EDITORIAL DIRECTOR *Belinda Gallagher*
ART DIRECTOR *Jo Cowan*
EDITOR *Carly Blake*
DESIGNERS *Michelle Cannatella, Joe Jones*
JUNIOR DESIGNER *Kayleigh Allen*
COVER DESIGNER *Joe Jones*
CONSULTANT *Janet Dyson*
PRODUCTION MANAGER *Elizabeth Collins*
REPROGRAPHICS *Stephan Davis, Ian Paulyn*

ISBN 978-1-84810-396-2

Printed in China

British Library Cataloguing-in-Publication Data
A catalogue record for this book is available from the British Library

ACKNOWLEDGEMENTS
The publishers would like to thank the following artists
who have contributed to this book:

The Bright Agency Katriona Chapman, Giuliano Ferri,
Mélanie Florian (inc. cover)

Advocate Art Andy Catling, Alida Massari

*The publishers would like to thank Robert Willoughby and
the London School of Theology for their help in compiling this book.*

Made with paper from a sustainable forest

www.mileskelly.net   info@mileskelly.net

www.factsforprojects.com

Self-publish your
children's book

buddingpress.co.uk

Contents

The Baby in the Basket

The seven-year famine happened just as Pharaoh's dream predicted, and in this time Joseph made amends with his brothers. His family came to live with him in Egypt, where his father Jacob lived out the rest of his years, and Joseph's brothers went on to have many children, grandchildren and great-grandchildren.

They did well in farming and business and became wealthy and powerful. As time passed, the Egyptians began calling them Israelites after the special name God had given to Jacob. Years went by and the number of Israelites grew, and different pharaohs came and went. After four hundred years, one king became particularly worried because there were so many Israelites. He told his advisors, "I am worried that if there was ever a war, the Israelites might turn against us and join with our enemies to defeat Egypt. We must find a way to stop their numbers growing further and to make them less powerful."

Pharaoh decided on drastic action – he sent his soldiers to seize the Israelites and turn them into slaves. He set them to work,

labouring on building sites and in the fields.

But still the number of Israelites increased, and families spread further throughout Egypt. Furious, Pharaoh came up with an even more wicked plan. He ordered his soldiers to search out every newborn Israelite boy and kill them all!

Of course, many desperate families tried to hide their beloved babies. One woman, who already had a daughter, Miriam, and a son, Aaron, kept her newborn boy hidden for three months. But as time went on, he became bigger and noisier and harder to conceal. In the end, the desperate woman took a reed basket and covered it with tar so it was watertight. She gently laid her baby in it and took it down to the River Nile, setting it in the thick, tall grasses at the

water's edge so it wouldn't float away. She told Miriam to stay a little way off to see that the baby was alright.

It wasn't long before the little girl saw a grand procession making its way down to the river. Her eyes opened wide at the sight of a young woman in magnificent robes, splendid jewels and rich makeup, accompanied by many servants and slaves. It was the princess, coming to bathe! The little girl watched, hardly daring to breathe, as the princess caught sight of the basket in the rushes and sent a servant to bring it to her. As soon as the princess saw the baby boy inside, she realized that he must be an Israelite. As she lifted the baby up, he began to cry and her heart melted with pity for the hungry, helpless child. She decided to take the baby home and keep him.

Bravely, Miriam dared to approach the princess, curtseying low. "Would you like me to find an Israelite nurse to look after him, Your Highness?" she suggested nervously.

The princess was pleased, and the little girl dashed home and fetched her mother!

So the little boy was at first cared for by his real mother, then given the education of an Egyptian prince. For the princess loved him so much, she adopted him as her own son. She called him Moses, which means 'to draw out', because she had rescued him by having him drawn out of the water.

Exodus chapters 1, 2

The Burning Bush

Moses was brought up as Egyptian royalty, but he knew that he was an Israelite by birth. As he grew up, he found it unbearable that he was living a rich, comfortable life of freedom, while other Israelites suffered as Egyptian slaves. One day, when he was a young man, he saw an Egyptian guard savagely hitting an Israelite man, and something inside him snapped. Moses beat the guard off, leaving him lying dead at his feet. News of his crime quickly spread. Moses knew that even the princess would not be able to save him from a terrible punishment, perhaps even death. He had no choice but to run away.

Moses fled to a country called Midian and settled into the quiet life of a shepherd. He looked after the flocks belonging to a village priest named Jethro, and he married his daughter, Zipporah. Years came and went and Moses' former life as an Egyptian royal seemed like a dream.

One day, Moses was out with his sheep when he came upon a very strange sight. A bush was on fire, but the leaves and branches of the bush weren't burning away.

While Moses marvelled, a voice suddenly boomed, "Moses, come no closer to this holy place! I am God — the God of your fathers, Abraham, Isaac and Jacob."

Moses fell to the ground, covering his face in terror.

"I have seen how my people, the Israelites, suffer in Egypt," echoed the voice. "But I will free them from slavery and return them to Canaan, a land of plenty that I promised would be their own. I want you to return to Egypt and rescue my people. Convince them to follow you and demand Pharaoh to release them."

Moses was shocked. "No one will believe that my orders are from you, Lord," he protested.

God gave Moses three magic signs so that he could prove it. Firstly, if Moses threw his shepherd's staff onto the ground, it turned into a snake! As soon as he picked it up again, it turned back into wood. Secondly, if Moses thrust his hand into his robe, it came out covered with scales and sores of the disease leprosy! When he put it back again, it was healed and healthy. Lastly, God told Moses that if he poured some water from the River Nile onto the ground, it would turn into blood!

Moses was stunned, but even so, he was

13

still unsure. "How can I be a leader, Lord?" he argued. "I don't even like talking in public. I go red and can't get the words out. Isn't there someone else you can send?"

"I have already told your brother Aaron to come and find you – he can do the talking," insisted God.

Moses hurried home and explained to his wife and his father-in-law what he had been ordered to do. To Moses' great surprise, Jethro believed him. God reassured Moses that it was safe for him to return to Egypt as a new pharaoh had come to the throne. So he and his wife packed up and set off through the countryside.

As they neared Egypt, Aaron came out to meet them, just as God had promised. The long-lost brothers hurried to see the

Israelite elders straight away. While Aaron explained that God had told Moses to lead the Israelites out of slavery, Moses proved that his message was from God by demonstrating the three magic signs in front of everyone. How the Israelites gasped! They believed Moses and sent up prayers of thanks that God had sent them help.

Exodus chapters 2 to 4

The Nine Plagues of Egypt

As God had ordered, Moses and Aaron requested an audience with Pharaoh himself. They were summoned to appear in Pharaoh's magnificent courtroom, in front of all his guards, advisors and magicians. "We have come at God's command to ask that you set the people of Israel free!" the brothers dared to tell Pharaoh.

But Pharaoh just laughed and waved for Moses and Aaron to be taken away. Then he set the Israelites even tougher tasks to do, making their lives even harder and more miserable.

"I've made the situation worse!" Moses told God, but God insisted that he try again.

So once more Moses and Aaron went to see Pharaoh. This time Aaron threw down Moses' staff, which turned into a snake, wriggling on the floor. Pharaoh signalled to his magicians and they too threw their staffs onto the floor, which also turned into slithering snakes. Pharaoh didn't even care when Aaron's snake

swallowed up
all of the
magicians' snakes.
"Audience over," he
announced coldly.

Moses despaired, but God
told him what to do. Early
the next day, Moses and Aaron
went down to the River
Nile and waited for
Pharaoh to take
his morning
walk there. When
Pharaoh refused their demands,
Aaron hit the waters with the staff.
At once, the Nile
turned to blood. The
river ran red for seven

days – all the fish died and there was no water to drink.
Yet the cold-hearted king was unmoved.

Then Moses signalled Aaron to stretch the staff over the Nile, and millions of frogs came hopping out of every river, stream and pond in Egypt. Everywhere anyone looked there were frogs…

anything anyone touched had frogs on it… the people couldn't move for frogs!
Then Pharaoh sent for Moses.

"Tell your god to make this stop and I will let your people go."

Immediately, there were so many dead frogs that the Egyptians had to pile them into huge, stinking heaps.

Pharaoh went back on his word.

So God ordered Moses to tell Aaron to hit the ground with the staff. The dust swirled and billions of lice swarmed out of the ground and over Egypt. Soon, everything that had been slimy with leaping frogs was itching with biting lice.

But Pharaoh's heart was as hard as stone.

So God sent vast clouds of flies humming into Egypt. They darkened the skies and blanketed the ground, flying into people's heads, landing on their eyelids, fluttering up their nostrils. But not one fly entered the house of an Israelite.

Then Pharaoh summoned Moses. "I will do as you ask," he announced, "if your god rids us of these flies!"

Once again, as soon as the flies were gone, Pharaoh simply broke his promise.

So God sent a dreadful disease which wiped out every horse, camel, ox, goat and sheep in the land – except for those belonging to the Israelites.

Still, Pharaoh would not give in.

Then God told Moses and Aaron to take a handful of ashes and throw it up into the air. As the wind blew the ashes across Egypt, an awful sickness spread, which caused terrible boils to break out over every person and each remaining animal – unless they were Israelite.

It just made Pharaoh more determined.

So God told Moses to stretch his staff up to the heavens… Thunder crashed, lighting flashed and hail fell from the skies in mighty torrents, flattening trees and plants. Everywhere except in the fields belonging to the Israelites.

At last Pharaoh called Moses again. "Enough!" he spat. "Make it stop and I will do what you ask." Moses prayed and the storm calmed. "I lied," announced Pharaoh triumphantly. He turned on his heel and strode away.

The very next day, a strange wind blew across Egypt, thick with locusts. Within a few hours they had eaten every blade of grass, every leaf, every ear of corn, every fruit on the trees.

"Aaaaaaargh!" howled Pharaoh. "Alright, the Israelites can go." The wind changed direction and the locusts were blown into the Red Sea and drowned.

But still, Pharaoh did not go through with his promise. So God told Moses to stretch out his hand and Egypt was swamped in total darkness for three days and nights. As his miserable people stumbled around blindly and the country ground to a halt, Pharaoh once again summoned Moses. "The Israelites may go, and this time I will not go back on my word," he spat, his eyes full of hate. "As long as they leave all their sheep, goats, camels and donkeys.

Moses listened to God.

"No," he replied, and Pharaoh turned white with fury.

"Then get out," roared the cruel king. "Your people will be my slaves forever. If I ever lay eyes on you again, you will die!"

Exodus chapters 5 to 10

The First Passover

God spoke to Moses and said, "I am going to send one last plague upon Egypt, so terrible that Pharaoh will be glad to let the Israelites go. At midnight, every firstborn child in Egypt shall die. From the firstborn of Pharaoh to the firstborn of the lowliest servant to the firstborn of every animal. No one shall escape – unless they

are an Israelite. Here's what they have to do to be spared. Every family must cook a lamb and smear their doorposts with the blood. Then I shall know which houses are Israelite homes.

"Forever after, this day will be called Passover and celebrated as the first day of the year. By my passing over the land tonight, my people will be set free – the beginning of a new era."

Next morning, nothing could be heard in Egypt except for wailing and screaming as people discovered their loved ones were dead. People and animals had breathed their last in every household across the land – except for the homes of the Israelites.

Once again Moses and Aaron found themselves before Pharaoh, who was weeping over his own dead firstborn son.

"Take your people and go!" he whispered. "Be gone, and never darken my lands again."

All over Pharaoh's country, the doomed Egyptians were so desperate to be rid of the Israelites that they offered them gold, silver and jewels to leave right away.

And that is how over six hundred thousand men, women and children came to gather to walk out of Egypt. After over four hundred years of captivity, the Israelites were heading home.

Exodus chapters 11, 12

The Parting of the Red Sea

God Himself guided the Israelites as they travelled out of Egypt and into the wilderness beyond. By day He appeared as a column of cloud and by night, as a column of fire, so they could follow Him.

The Israelites had reached the sands of the Red Sea when they noticed a massive cloud of dust behind them in the distance, rushing towards them at great speed.

It was the Egyptian army! The minute that Pharaoh had ordered the Israelites to leave, he regretted his decision. In a whirlwind of hatred, he called for his best armour and ordered six hundred of his finest charioteers to make ready to chase after his former slaves.

The Israelites were terrified and turned on Moses. "Did you lead us out of captivity only to meet our deaths in the desert?" they cried.

"Don't be afraid," Moses told the Israelites. "The Lord will protect you, wait and see." And God spoke to Moses, telling him what to do.

With the Egyptian army thundering ever closer, Moses urged the Israelites forward –

straight towards the Red Sea. Then the column of cloud blew over Pharaoh and his charioteers, smothering them so they couldn't see their way ahead. While the bewildered, frustrated Egyptians were forced to slow their pace, Moses reached the foaming seashore and stretched out his hand towards the ocean.

An immense wind blew up, nearly sweeping the Israelites off their feet. It howled and hurled, and with great gusts this way and that it split the waves. The wind drove the waters to the right and left, higher and higher, until they rolled back leaving a wide pathway of seabed in between. Then bravely and boldly, Moses strode down the sand, leading the Israelites between the towering walls of water on either side.

Then came the Egyptian army,
galloping forwards. How petrified they were
when they saw the waters of the Red Sea
divided in front of them. Yet they plunged
into the passage as the last of the Israelites

reached the sandy shore on the other side.

As Pharaoh and his charioteers sped ever closer to the Israelites, Moses stretched out his hand once more. Then the towering walls of water teetered, toppled and crashed down. The Red Sea closed over the Egyptians, drowning each and every one, and the Israelites were truly free at last.

Exodus chapters 13, 14

The Ten Commandments

The Israelites trusted Moses and followed him uncomplainingly into the hot, rocky desert. After three months, the Israelites arrived at the foot of the holy mountain of Sinai. Moses announced they would camp there a while. He told them that they should make ready with prayers and rituals because in three days' time God

was going to speak to all of them.

Sure enough, on the morning of the third day, black storm clouds gathered around the peak of the mountain, hiding it from view. Thunder rumbled and lightning split the skies. Then the earth shook, and the mountain began to spew out flames and smoke as if it were an enormous furnace. A sound like a giant trumpet blared out through the air, calling the terrified Israelites to assemble at the foot of the mountain. Then Moses slowly climbed up and up towards the smoking, fiery mountain-top and disappeared from view into the clouds.

For a long time after he had gone, thunder continued to echo around the slopes and many Israelites thought it was the voice of God talking to their leader. When the noise had at last died away, Moses came back down the mountain and announced that God had given him ten important rules of behaviour:

1. *You should not worship any other god but me.*

2. *You should not make a statue or a picture to worship.*

3. *You should only use my name respectfully.*

4. *You should keep the seventh day, or Sabbath, of every week as a holy day of rest.*

5. *You should always be respectful to your parents.*

6. *You should never commit murder.*

7. *You should never be unfaithful to your partner.*

8. *You should not steal.*

9. *You should not lie.*

10. *You should not envy the things that other people have.*

Moses wrote the Ten Commandments down, and lots of lesser rules too. The very

next day he built an altar at the foot of the mountain and asked the Israelites to vow to obey the rules. Then Moses made a sacrifice to seal their solemn promise.

Yet God still had more that He wanted the Israelites to learn, so He summoned Moses up the mountain once more, where they could talk on their own together. The Israelites watched as their leader climbed up the mountain one more time and disappeared alone into the dark clouds.

The Israelites watched and waited for Moses to return… watched and waited for seven long weeks, but there was no sign of their leader. Worried and confused, they came to the conclusion that God had abandoned them and Moses would never return.

"Make something for us to worship," they begged Aaron. "We need something we can see and touch." Thousands of men and women brought Aaron their gold jewellery. He melted it down and made an enormous statue of a calf, one of the animals that was sometimes sacrificed to God. To please the people and keep them under control, Aaron even built the calf an enormous altar and declared there would be a festival in its honour.

The people were delighted. At last they had a straightforward god. One that wasn't

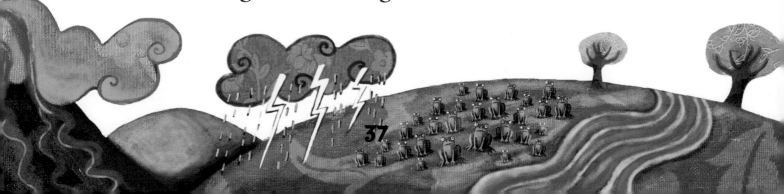

invisible and didn't speak to them in thunder, giving them complicated lists of things they should and shouldn't do. Immediately, the Israelites began praying to the calf and offering it sacrifices, and singing and dancing around it.

As they did so, Moses came clambering down the mountainside at last. He held two huge stone tablets on which God Himself had written out the ten most important commandments so that no one could forget them or get them wrong.

Moses knew already about how the Israelites were worshipping the golden calf because God had told him while they were up the mountain. God had been full of fury and so was Moses. Enraged at the sight that met his eyes as he approached the camp, he flung the stone tablets to the ground and they shattered into pieces. Then he hurled the golden calf into the flames of one of the sacrificial fires.

"Aaron, what did everyone do to you that you allowed this to happen?" Moses spat with disgust at his brother. Then he called for anyone who was on God's side to go and stand next to him. Only the men of the tribe of Levi took up places next to Moses. On God's orders, he told each of them to grab a sword and put to death everyone who stood in their way as punishment for their sins.

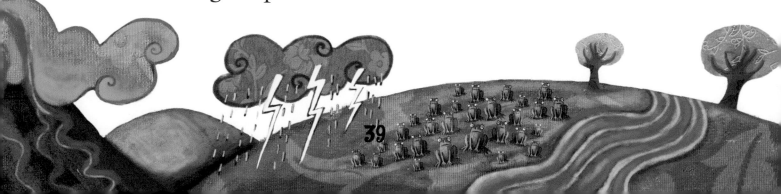

39

Over three thousand Israelites were killed that night. The next day, Moses went back up the mountain to pray to God for forgiveness for the wickedness of His Chosen People.

Exodus chapters 19 to 24, 32